Look What Came From

Spain

by
Kevin Davis

LEE

Franklin Watts
A Division of Scholastic Inc.
New York Toronto London Auckland Sydney
Mexico City New Delhi Hong Kong
Danbury, Connecticut

Series Concept: Shari Joffe
Design: Steve Marton

Library of Congress Cataloging-in-Publication Data

Davis, Kevin A.
    Look what came from Spain / by Kevin Davis.
        p. cm. — (Look what came from)
Includes bibliographical references and index.
Summary: Describes the many things that originally came
from Spain, such as inventions, holidays, animals, foods,
sports, and music.
    ISBN 0-531-11962-9 (lib. bdg.) 0-531-16629-5 (pbk.)
    1. Spain—Civilization—Juvenile literature.
2. Civilization, Modern—Spanish influences—Juvenile
literature. [1. Civilization, Modern—Spanish influences.
2. Spain—Civilization.] I. Look what came from series.
    DP48 .D28 2001
    946—dc21

                                    2001046797

Photographs © 2002: A Perfect Exposure/Michelle Chaplow: 11 right, 15 left;
Bridgeman Art Library International Ltd., London/New York: 6 top
(Mithra-Index), 20 left (The British Sporting Art Trust); Corbis Images:
14 (Archivo Iconografico, S.A.), 18 (Owen Franken); Dave G. Houser/
HouserStock, Inc.: 8 right; David R. Frazier: 10 left; International Stock
Photo/Roberto Arakaki: 9 left, 25 right; Iva Jarova: 20 right, 21 left;
Mansell Collection: 7; Mercury Press/Isaac Hernandez: back cover, 4, 9
center, 11 top left, 13 bottom right, 23 left; Nance S. Trueworthy: 27 top
right, 27 top left, 27 bottom; Peter Arnold Inc./Walter H. Hodge: 32;
PhotoEdit/Bill Aron: cover top, 6 bottom; Photo Researchers, NY: 21 right
(William D. Bachman), 24 (Robert Frerck), 10 right, 11 bottom left (Andrew
J. Martinez), 23 right (Hans Reinhard/OKAPIA); Robert Fried Photography:
cover left, 3, 8 left, 15 right, 19; Superstock, Inc.: cover background, inside
borders, 9 right, 22, 25 left; The Image Works/Stuart Cohen: 16; Woodfin
Camp & Associates: 12, 13 top and left (Chuck Fishman), 17 (Robert Frerck).

Map on page 5 by Lisa Jordan.

Contents

Greetings from Spain! 4

Inventions 6

Music 8

Food 10

Customs 14

Sports 16

Animals 20

Festivals 24

A Craft from Spain 26

How Do You Say . . . ? 28

To Find Out More 29

Glossary 30

Index 31

Greetings from Spain!

Spain is a big and beautiful country in western Europe. Lots of great things come from Spain, from delicious foods to lively music and dance. Spain is located on the Iberian Peninsula, a large body of land that sticks out below France.

The flag of Spain

People have lived in Spain for many thousands of years. The earliest people to live in Spain were known as the Iberians. The country had many wars during its history, and different groups of people settled in Spain, including the ancient Romans and the Moors (Muslim people who came from North Africa).

Today, Spain is a very diverse country with three main regions, each of which has its own culture and variations in language. The main language in Spain is Spanish. The word for "friend" in Spanish is *amigo*. So come on, *amigo*, let's take a look at what comes from Spain!

castanets

quill pen

Merino sheep

Madrid
★

FRANCE

Barcelona

Atlantic Ocean

Portugal

SPAIN

Paella

Mediterranean Sea

siesta

N

Morocco

Inventions

Have you ever seen a pen made out of a big feather? This is known as a **quill pen,** believed to have originated in Spain about 1,400 years ago. A quill pen has a hollow shaft that holds ink and a sharp point for writing. People don't use them much today because we now have better pens. The quill pen led to the invention of the modern ink pen, which is much easier and less messy to use!

Quill pen

Painting from the 1500s showing a Spanish man using a quill pen

Before the first submarine was invented, people were looking for ways to work underwater. In Spain, some people built a big thing called a **diving bell.** The first one was made in 1538. It was a bell-shaped device made of leather and metal and was lowered over the person to keep the water out. Nearly 100 years later, someone invented a system to pump air into the diving bell so people could breathe inside of it longer.

The first diving bell

Flamenco dancer in Seville, Spain

Flamenco musician

Music

Flamenco is a very popular type of music in Spain. Many people mistakenly believe flamenco is a dance. People dance to flamenco music, which is performed by a guitarist and singer. People often clap their hands and stomp their feet to the music. Children learn to dance to this music at neighborhood festivals.

Flamenco music is thought to have been developed by the Moors, who brought it to Spain from North Africa in the early A.D. 700s. It is a very dramatic type of music and varies from region to region in Spain.

Castanets

Spanish girl using castanets

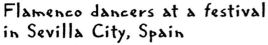
Flamenco dancers at a festival in Sevilla City, Spain

Flamenco dancers and players often use percussion instruments called **castanets.** These look like two clam shells and are usually made of wood. They make a loud clicking sound when hit together.

9

Man cooking paella

Food

Some of the most delicious foods in the world come from Spain. Each region of the country has its own specialty. People in Spain eat two main meals: lunch and dinner. Breakfast is usually very small.

Gazpacho

One of the most famous dishes from Spain is **paella.** This tasty meal is made with lots of ingredients, including saffron rice, vegetables, seafood, and meat. Paella originated in Valencia, the main rice-growing region of Spain.

Most people think of soup as a food that is hot. Spain, however, is famous for a cold soup—**gazpacho.** This refreshing soup is made from chopped tomatoes, peppers, cucumbers, olive oil, vinegar, and spices. It is great on hot summer days!

Paella

Man pouring sherry from a keg

A well-known type of wine called **sherry** also comes from Spain. It is a sweet wine that people like to sip. It is also used for cooking.

more food

Various tapas

People in Spain also like to snack on small servings of food called **tapas.** Today, tapas restaurants are popular all over the world. At a tapas restaurant, people order several small samples of dishes, such as marinated and grilled meats, small pieces of fish, potato salad with garlic mayonnaise, and croquettes (small pastries filled with meat).

For breakfast or lunch, people in Spain enjoy a special omelet called a **tortilla Española.** This dish is made with eggs and potatoes and is served like a pie. It may also have meat or vegetables inside.

Tortilla Española

13

Customs

One of the oldest customs in Spain is the siesta. During a siesta, people stop working and take a break to have lunch and sometimes a nap. This custom began because afternoons are very hot in Spain, so it is a difficult time to work.

Families often gather at home during the siesta to have a big lunch and spend time together. Then, after a short nap, people go back to work late in the afternoon, when it is cooler. The siesta lasts about three hours.

Painting showing people in Spain taking a siesta in the 1800s

People in Spain taking a paseo

Some people in Spain like to take a nice leisurely walk late in the day with their families and friends. This tradition is known as the **paseo,** and is popular in many other Spanish-speaking countries as well. The paseo usually begins in the late afternoon. People walk, shop, have snacks, and stroll through the center of town.

15

Sports

Bullfighting has been a popular sport in Spain for thousands of years. Many people in Spain consider it to be a contest of art and great skill. But others believe it is a cruel sport because it involves killing the bull.

In Spain, bullfights are called *corridas*. They are held in large arenas called bull rings. The matador is the main challenger against the bull. He dresses in a colorful costume and wears a black hat with three corners.

During the contest, the matador uses a red cape to get the bull to charge as close to him as possible. When this happens, the crowd often yells *"olé!"* At the end of the contest, the matador kills the bull with a sword.

A matador and bull

Bullfight in Spain

more sports

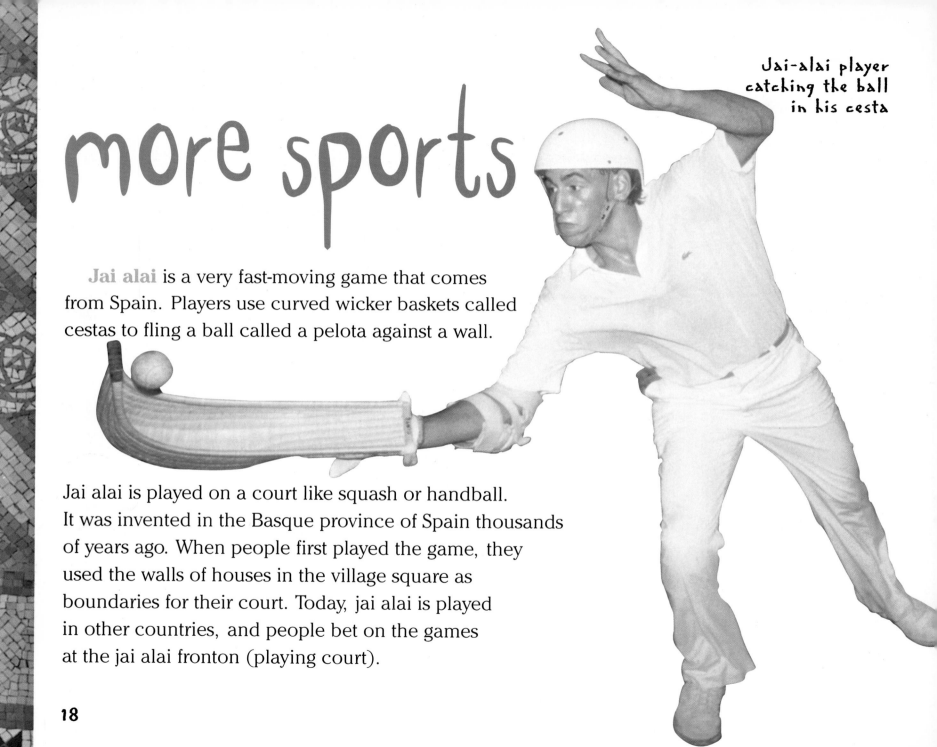

Jai-alai player
catching the ball
in his cesta

Jai alai is a very fast-moving game that comes from Spain. Players use curved wicker baskets called cestas to fling a ball called a pelota against a wall.

Jai alai is played on a court like squash or handball. It was invented in the Basque province of Spain thousands of years ago. When people first played the game, they used the walls of houses in the village square as boundaries for their court. Today, jai alai is played in other countries, and people bet on the games at the jai alai fronton (playing court).

Men playing jai-alai

Animals

Some of the friendliest breeds of dogs come from Spain. They are called **spaniels.** These dogs were first used to help hunters scare animals out from the woods or bushes. Many modern breeds of spaniels were developed in Britain. The Cocker spaniel is one of the most popular.

Another dog from Spain is the **Spanish mastiff.** It was once used as a military dog because of its fighting ability. Today, it is a popular family pet in Spain. Its coat is usually red, and it is a very loyal and reliable companion.

Painting showing spaniels in the 1800s

20

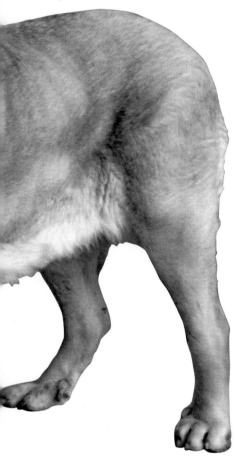

Spanish mastiff

Merino sheep

Merino sheep, which come from Spain, produce some of the softest wool in the world. Because the wool is so long, fine, and silky, it makes very comfortable sweaters and is commonly used in fine clothing.

more animals

An excellent riding horse also comes from Spain. The **Andalusian** is strong and handsome. It was favored among wealthy people in the 1500s and 1600s. This horse is usually gray and has a large mane and tail. It is believed that Andalusians are descended from horses from Syria or North Africa.

Andalusian horses at a horse fair in Spain

Spanish lynx

Spanish wildcat

The Spanish lynx is a beautiful and rare cat that lives in the wild in Spain. Its coat varies from yellow and gray to cinnamon red. It has spots on its sides and feet and has a tail with a black tip. This cat, which is protected in Spain's national parks, is an excellent climber.

The Spanish wildcat looks like a big tabby cat, but also lives in the wild. It is similar to wildcats that live throughout Europe. This cat was long hunted for its pelts or killed because it preyed on livestock. Today, the Spanish wildcat survives only in isolated areas.

Festivals

The running of the bulls in Pamplona

People in Spain love to celebrate. There are many festivals and holidays with parades, dancing, and great foods.

One of the most famous festivals is the **running of the bulls.** This event occurs on St. Fermin's Day in July in the northern town of Pamplona. Bulls are let loose at the entrance of the city and people run in front of or along with the bulls through the narrow streets toward the bull arena. It is very exciting, but also very dangerous. Sometimes, people get hurt by the bulls.

24

The tomato-throwing
festival in Buñol

One of the silliest events in Spain is the tomato-throwing festival in the town of Buñol, outside of Valencia. This messy party, called *La Fiesta de Tomatina,* is held to celebrate the delicious, juicy tomatoes of that region. People gather in the streets and throw over-ripe tomatoes at each other. This is done in good fun and is not meant to hurt anyone. It's quite a sight!

25

A Craft from Spain

If you want your house or clothing to smell really nice, you can make a Spanish orange pomander to hang on the wall or put in your closet. A pomander is made with a dried orange and a mixture of spices. It's very easy to make.

Spanish orange pomander

You'll need:
- 1 fresh orange, Spanish if possible
- 1/4-inch-wide tape
- 1/4-inch-wide ribbon
- toothpick
- cloves
- paper lunch bag
- two teaspoons of ground cinnamon
- 1 tablespoon of orrisroot (available from health-food stores or drug stores)

1. Wrap tape around the orange, as shown in the photograph on opposite page.

2. Pierce the orange skin with the toothpick and push a clove, pointed end first, into the hole. Cover all four sections of the orange with cloves the same way. Do not put cloves into the orange in the areas covered with tape.

3. Tip the cinnamon and orrisroot powder into the paper bag. Shake the bag to mix the powders. Drop in the orange and

continue shaking the bag until the orange is covered with the mixture. Leave the orange in the bag in a warm, dry place for about five weeks.

4. Take out the orange. Blow away the excess powder and remove the tape. Tie the ribbon along the rows left by the tape and hang the pomander on the wall, on a windowsill, or near your clothes. The pomander will make your room and clothes smell fresh and fruity, and it wards off moths.

How do you say....?

Spanish is the main language in Spain. Try saying some words in Spanish for yourself!

English	Spanish	How to pronounce it
good morning	buenos días	BWAY-nohs DEE-ahs
goodbye	adiós	ah-dee-OHS
bull	toro	TOE-roh
cat	gato	GAH-toe
dance	baile	BYE-lay
dog	perro	PAY-roh
horse	caballo	ka-BYE-yoh
pen	pluma	PLOO-mah
soup	sopa	SOH-pah
sport	juego	HWAY-goh
tomato	tomate	toe-MAHT-tay

To find out more

Here are some other resources to help you learn more about Spain:

Books

Goodwin, Bob. **A Taste of Spain.** Raintree/Steck Vaughn, 2000.

Knorr, Rosanne, and Knorr, John. **If I Lived in Spain.** Longstreet Press, 1994.

Kohen, Elizabeth Robin. **Spain** (Cultures of the World series). Benchmark Books, 1995.

Rogers, Lura. **Spain** (Enchantment of the World, Second Series). Children's Press, 2001.

Selby, Anna. **Spain** (Country Fact Files). Raintree/Steck Vaughn, 1994.

Spain: In Pictures (Visual Geography series). Lerner Publications, 1995.

Organizations and Online Sites

Spain Tourism
http://www.tourspain.es/turespai/marcoi.htm
Provides information about cities, arts, Spanish culture, sports, beaches, environment, business travel, and places to stay.

Spain: Virtual Journey
http://www.ontheline.org.uk/explore/journey/spain/spindex.htm
Explore daily life in Spain and cultural traditions such as bullfights, flamenco, Spanish food, and more. Check out the guidebook for facts and figures too.

Spain: World Sites Atlas
http://www.sitesatlas.com/Europe/Spain/spamain.htm
A collection of general and tourist information, plus Web links, maps, and photos of places in Spain.

Glossary

boundary something that marks or shows a limit or end

culture the beliefs and customs of a group of people that are passed from one generation to another

descended to have come down from a certain source

diverse varied

fling to hurl in the air

isolated alone; far away from people

leisurely slow, done without hurry

marinated soaked in a sauce for flavor

originated to have come from

pelts animal skins

peninsula body of land that extends from a larger body of land

percussion instrument musical instrument sounded by striking

preyed hunted

shaft a long, usually rounded slender part

squash game played with a racket and ball on a court with four walls

tradition custom or activity handed down from generation to generation

wicker thin, flexible twig used to make baskets

Index

ancient Romans, 4

Andalusian horse, 22

Basque province, 18

bullfighting, 16

Buñol, 25

castanets, 9

cesta, 18

diving bell, 7

Flamenco, 8

fronton, 18

gazpacho, 11

jai alai, 18

matador, 16

Merino sheep, 21

Moors, 4, 8

paella, 11

Pamplona, 24

paseo, 15

pelota, 18

quill pen, 6

running of the bulls, 24

sherry, 11

siesta, 14

spaniels, 20

Spanish language, 28

Spanish lynx, 23

Spanish mastiff, 20

Spanish orange pomander, 26

Spanish wildcat, 23

tapas, 12

tomato-throwing festival, 25

tortilla Española, 13

Valencia, 11, 25

Look what doesn't come from Spain!

Spanish moss, also called black moss, is a silvery-gray plant that grows in the woods on other plants. It is found in North America, South America, Central America, and the West Indies—but not in Spain!

Spanish moss

Meet the Author

Kevin Davis loves to travel and write about the interesting places he has visited. He lives in Chicago. This book is dedicated to his friends Andy Martin, Trevor Jensen, and Jon Marcus, who visited Spain with Kevin.